Seesaws
Nutcrackers
Brooms

Seesaws
Nutcrackers
Brooms

SIMPLE MACHINES
THAT ARE REALLY
LEVERS

BY CHRISTOPHER LAMPTON
PICTURES BY CAROL NICKLAUS

THE MILLBROOK PRESS · BROOKFIELD, CT
A GATEWAY BOOK

Cataloging-in-Publication Data

Lampton, Christopher
Seesaws, Nutcrackers and brooms / Christopher
Lampton; pictures by Carol Nicklaus. Brookfield,
CT., Millbrook Press, 1991.
32 p. : ill.
Includes glossary and index.
ISBN 1-878841-22-X
1. Simple Machines. 2. Levers.
3. Science - Experiments. I. Title. II. Carol Nicklaus, ill.

Seesaws
Nutcrackers
Brooms

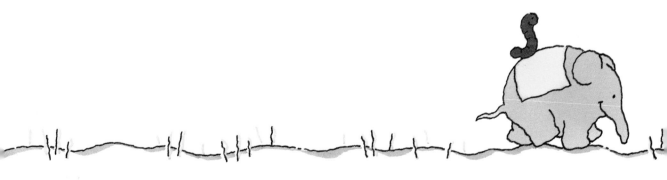

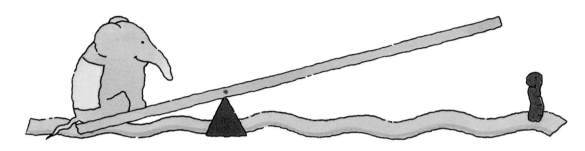

Look around you. How many machines can you see?

There's the dishwasher in your kitchen, the car in your garage, and the lawn mower in your yard, to mention only a few.

Machines are everywhere because we depend on machines to do things we couldn't do without them.

The dishwasher, car, and lawn mower are **complex machines.** They are made up of many parts that work together in complicated ways. Some run on electricity. Some use gasoline. Some are operated by a person turning a wheel or crank.

SIMPLE MACHINES

PULLEY

INCLINED PLANE

Complex machines are made up of different kinds of **simple machines.** Simple machines do not have many parts. Inclined planes, pulleys, wheels and axles, and levers are all simple machines.

When you use a simple machine, you can't just turn it on as you would a dishwasher or a clothes dryer. You have to put forth effort to get work done. What the simple machine does is allow you to do things you might not be able to do otherwise.

A lever is a simple machine that can help you accomplish a variety of tasks. Seesaws, nutcrackers, and brooms are three different kinds of levers. You can use a seesaw as a lever to help you lift a heavy friend up in the air—something you could not do at all without this simple machine. With a nutcracker you can crack the hard shell of a nut, a job that most of us could not do with our bare hands. And a broom helps you sweep a large area with only small movements of your hands, a far easier task than kneeling on the floor to brush the dust from each small area.

Let's look first at a seesaw.

WHEEL
AND
AXLE

LEVER

(9)

A seesaw is a board on a stand. A seesaw acts as a lever when you use it to lift a friend who is much larger than you. If you tried to lift this friend with only your arms, you probably could not do it. A seesaw will not only help you lift your larger friend, it will also be easy and fun!

Look at this seesaw to see the three parts that are found in all levers:

▲ The top of the stand is the **fulcrum.**

▲ The lengths of board between the stand and each end of the seesaw are the **lever arms.**

▲ Your friend is the **load.**

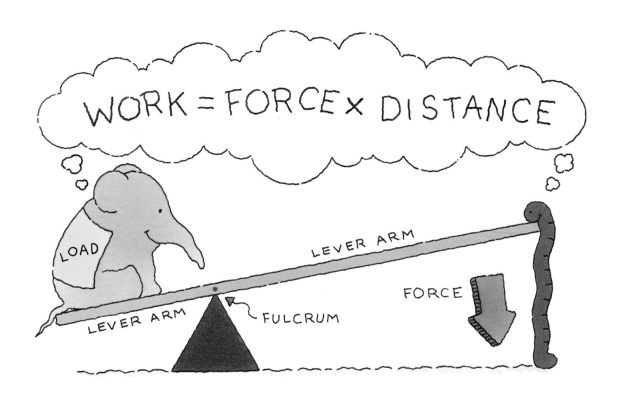

You might wonder why a seesaw is a machine, and how playing on it can be called work. Well, scientists have a very special way of defining work. They measure the amount of force you must use to move something and how far you must move to do it. Then they multiply these two measurements (force × distance) to define how much work has been done. So, when you lift your friend on a seesaw, you are using the seesaw to do what scientists call work.

Now let's explore why using a lever can make it easier to lift your friend.

Place a ruler on a table so that the first 4 inches hang over the edge of the table. Now place an apple on the ruler's 12-inch mark. Press down on the end of the ruler until the apple begins to lift off the table. Notice how hard you have to push to lift the apple.

Now slide the ruler toward you until the 8-inch mark is at the edge of the table. Push down on the ruler until the apple lifts off the table. It didn't take as much effort to lift the apple this time, did it? Congratulations! You have just used a lever to make your job easier.

The edge of the table was the fulcrum. The two sections of the ruler on either side of the fulcrum were the lever arms. The apple was the load. By pushing down on the ruler, you exerted a force, called the **effort.**

You must have noticed that the closer the apple was to the edge of the table, the easier it was to push the ruler down and lift the apple up. This demonstrates a very important point about how a lever works: the closer the fulcrum is to the load, the less effort you have to use to lift the load. So, the closer the fulcrum (the edge of the table) was to the load (the weight of the apple as it sat on the edge of the ruler), the less effort (pushing down on the ruler) you had to use.

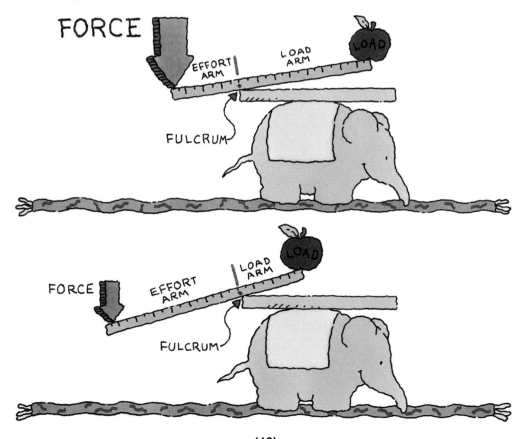

Repeat the apple and ruler experiments again, this time noticing not only how hard you have to push to move the apple, but also how *far* you have to push. When you have the ruler's 8-inch mark at the edge of the table, you don't have to push very hard to move the apple up one inch into the air, but you do have to push the long end of the ruler quite a way down below the edge of the table.

On the other hand, when you adjust the ruler so that you are pushing down on the 4-inch portion, you have to push much harder—but you do not have to push the ruler down very far.

Remember how scientists define work—the amount of force (how hard you had to push on the ruler) times the distance (how far down you had to push the ruler) is equal to the amount of work accomplished (how high you were able to lift the apple).

The next time you are at a playground, think about the work that you want to accomplish on a seesaw. What could you do to the seesaw to make your work easier? If you can't adjust the seesaw, would it help to ask your friend to move? Hint: repeat the apple and ruler experiments, pretending that your friend is the apple.

When you use a lever to perform work, you are really trading effort (how hard you push down on the ruler) for distance (how far you move the load). If you push down on the long end of the ruler, you use less effort, but you have to push farther. A lever works best when it lets you use a comfortable amount of force and distance to do a task. When a machine lets us use less effort to move a load, we say that the machine gives us a **mechanical advantage.**

You can use mechanical advantage for more practical tasks than lifting an apple. Take another kind of lever—a crowbar, for example. You can pry a big rock from the ground by sticking one end of the crowbar under the rock (the load). You brace the crowbar against the ground or against a small rock placed next to the big rock. (The ground or the small rock is the fulcrum.) Then you push down (the effort) on the other end of the crowbar. With a crowbar you can move a rock you couldn't budge with your bare hands.

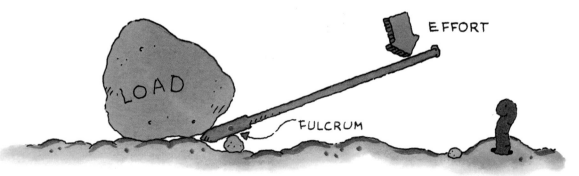

And how about the can opener you use to punch a hole in a juice can? In this lever, the edge of the can is the fulcrum. By pulling the end of the opener upward a long distance, you push the pointed end downward only a short distance. But you pierce right through the metal on the top of the can. Try doing that without a mechanical advantage!

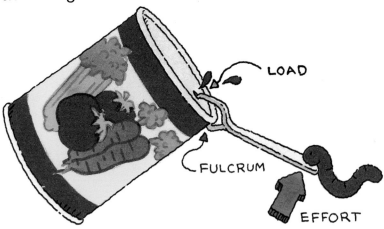

The crowbar and the can opener are called first-class levers. This means that the fulcrum lies between the effort and the load. And when you lifted the apple with the ruler, you used a first-class lever too. The edge of the table (the fulcrum) was between the effort (your hand pushing the ruler down) and the load (the apple).

There are two other kinds of levers. A wheelbarrow is an example of what is called a second-class lever. Like a first-class lever, a wheelbarrow has a fulcrum, an effort, and a load. But they are in different places. In a second-class lever, the load is in the middle, between the fulcrum and the effort. A wheelbarrow's load is in the barrow, between the wheel (the fulcrum) and your grip on the handle (the effort).

You gain a mechanical advantage when you use a second-class lever just as you do when you use a first-class lever. The closer the load is to the fulcrum, and the farther away the effort, the less effort you need to lift the load. When you use a wheelbarrow, your hands (the effort) are a lot farther away from the fulcrum (the wheel) than whatever is in the barrow (the load).

A nutcracker is a double second-class lever. It has two lever arms joined at a hinge. To crack a nut, you put the nut (the load) between the hinge (the fulcrum) and your hand (the effort). Like a wheelbarrow, the nutcracker's effort and load lie on the same side of the fulcrum.

Place a hard nut between the arms of the nutcracker. First, squeeze the arms with your hands close to the nut. Can you crack it? Then, place your hands at the ends of the arms. Is it easier this way? You bet! And the longer the arms, the easier it is to cra-a-a-ack the nut!

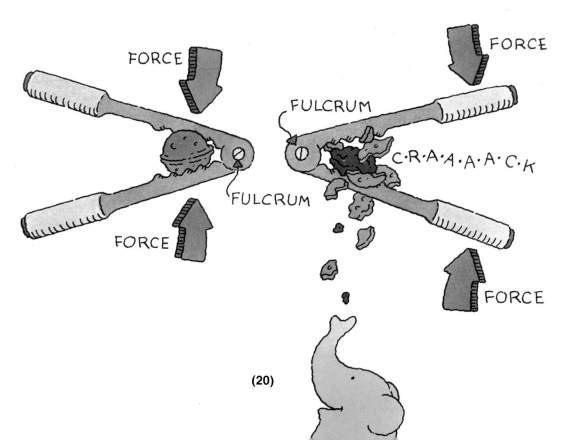

FORCE

FORCE

FULCRUM

FORCE

FULCRUM

C·R·A·A·A·A·C·K

FORCE

A broom is a third-class lever. It's different from either a first-class or a second-class lever. The broom's effort is between the fulcrum and the load.

One hand holds the broom steady at the top of the handle. That hand acts as the fulcrum. The dirt you push is your load. Your other hand (the effort) is usually near the middle of the broom handle. That hand moves the bristles that sweep the floor.

You aren't trying to lift something with a broom, so your muscles don't need the extra help that a first-class or second-class lever gives them. Instead, you gain speed and distance when you use the broom as a third-class lever. The broom's bristles quickly move the dust a long distance across the floor while your hand moves the broom a lesser distance at a slower speed.

Surely you've noticed by now that when you use a simple machine there is always a trade-off. To use less force to move the apple, you had to push the ruler down a longer distance. What did you trade off to gain the extra distance and speed at the end of the broom? You probably didn't notice because the load was so light, but you used more force to move the load than you would have used with your bare hands. To gain the distance at the end of the broom where the load is, you lost much of the force you applied at the point of effort.

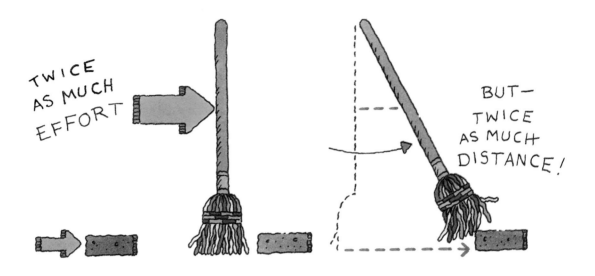

TWICE AS MUCH EFFORT

BUT— TWICE AS MUCH DISTANCE!

You will feel this trade-off if you try to sweep something heavy, like a brick or a book. Hold the top of the broom with one hand (the fulcrum). Placing your other hand about half way down the broom, use it to exert a force (the effort). Did you notice that you had to push about twice as hard to move the brick than if you simply pushed it along the ground with your hand?

You have to push harder to move the brick with the broom because you trade most of your broom-pushing effort for distance and speed. You slowly move your hand a short distance while the brick moves rapidly over a much longer distance. This is an example of trade-off. Your extra effort is traded for distance and speed.

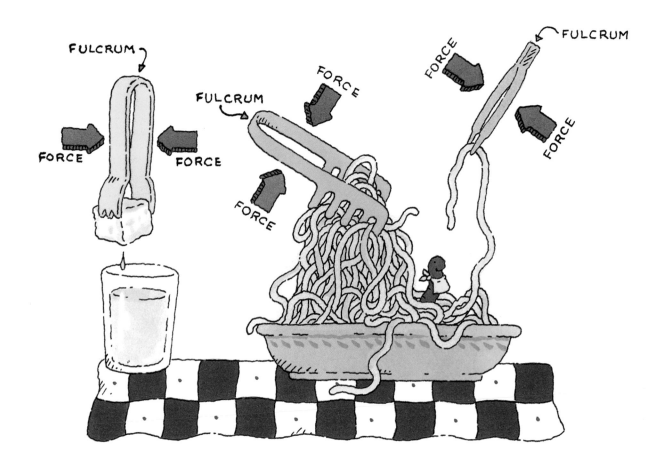

There are double third-class levers as well. Remember that in a third-class lever, the effort goes between the fulcrum and the load. Ice tongs and tweezers are both double third-class levers. You squeeze (the effort) in the middle of the ice tongs, and the tongs grip (the load) the ice. The fulcrum is the closed end of the tongs.

Levers are parts of many complex machines.

Take an automobile, for instance. The mechanism that steers the front wheels of the car contains levers. In many cars the handle of the emergency brake is a lever. Certain door handles are levers. Turn signals often operate with levers. The accelerator is a lever. And levers connect windshield wipers to their source of power. You certainly couldn't drive very far without the help of this simple machine!

Even your own body works like a machine in many ways. Your jaw, for instance, is a kind of second-class lever. Like a nutcracker, it can crush food. Like the nutcracker's hinge, the joint that connects your jaw to your skull is the fulcrum. Powerful muscles supply the force that crushes the loads of food you put in your mouth.

Muscles also power your arm, which is a third-class lever. Your elbow acts as a fulcrum, and whatever you lift in your hand is the load.

You might say that machines copy nature. Natural levers have existed for millions of years. (Dinosaurs had powerful jaws!)

Can you name the levers shown here? Do you know what you'd use them for?

What kinds of levers are they? Which are first-class levers? Which are second-class levers? Which are third-class levers?

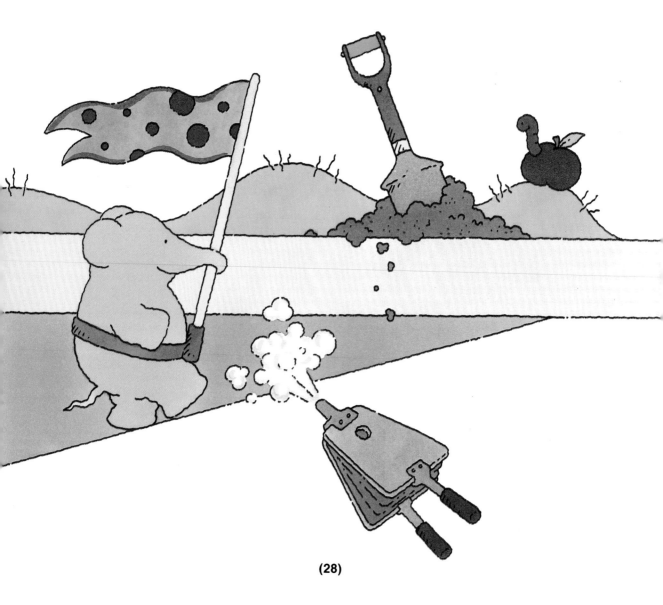

First-class levers: the oars and shovel.
Second-class levers: the joystick, bellows, and bottle opener.
Third-class levers: the fishing pole and parade flag.

About 2,000 years ago, a Greek scientist and philosopher named Archimedes explained how levers work. He said, "Give me a lever long enough and a place to stand and I will move the earth."

Well, nobody's done that yet. (What would you use for a fulcrum?) But we're still finding new ways to use levers.

Index / Glossary

Complex machine: a machine made up of combinations of simple machines, 8.

Effort: the force we apply to do work, 12.

Force: the effort applied to move something, 11.

Fulcrum: the point where a lever pivots, 10.

Lever: a simple machine made up of lever arms and fulcrum, 10.

Load: the force that resists the effort, 10.

Mechanical advantage: the relationship between the effort you put into the machine and the force you get out of it, 16.

Simple machine: a device that allows us to reduce the amount of effort we use to do work, 8–9.

Trade-off: the exchange between distance and force that occurs when we do work, 22–23.

Work: force times distance equals work, 15.